THE VALUES WORKBOOK

CREATING PERSONAL TRUTH AT WORK

ROBERT RABBIN AND JO HILLYARD

FORE THOUGHTS

Foster City, CA

Cover design by Suzanne Hannah Premo

Library of Congress Catalog Card Number: 97-90947

ISBN: 0-9659806-5-0

Printed in the United States of America
10 9 8 7 6 5 4 3 2 1

This book is available at special quantity discounts.
For information, contact Fore Thoughts,
969 G Edgewater Blvd., Suite 217, Foster City, CA 94404
Phone 800.571.0854 or Fax 650.345.4552

This book materialized in four phases: *serendipity, spontaneity, vision,* and *collaboration.*

Serendipity—

During a meeting in the summer of 1996 a client asked Rob to think about creating a seminar based on Rob's consulting principles.

Spontaneity—

A few days later, never having previously reflected on *how* he did what he did, Rob wrote out twenty-five principles which he entitled *Consulting: The Path of Service.* That document took five hours to write and was almost 6,000 words in length. It simply flowed out of a silent inquiry into his style of consulting.

Vision—

Rob sent his manuscript to Jo, a friend and colleague. She immediately saw its value and proposed converting the principles into a workbook. Jo's vision was seen through twenty years of experience as a training consultant for corporations.

Collaboration—

In their subsequent collaboration, the original manuscript was edited and modified into its present format. They wanted to expand the original focus of the work, believing it had a more universal appeal and application. The authors felt that every person—regardless of profession—could benefit by reflecting on *how* they do what they do, and that this process would reveal ways in which the "lightning" of passion, truth, and meaning could be caught in the jar of the "workplace."

CONTENTS

INTRODUCTION

For some time now corporations and organizations in both the public and private sectors have been working to define the values upon which they operate. Explicit values announce to employees, stockholders, vendors, customers and the community *how* that organization intends to do business. Agreed-upon values also help organizations navigate the sometimes complex crosscurrents of opportunity and integrity, of profit and social responsibility, of growth and quality.

Business professionals are also finding a need to clarify the values upon which they professionally engage with others. It is no longer enough to "have a job"; many people are seeking a fuller life at work, one that is consistent with the larger focus of their lives. It is common to hear workplace discussions of "meaning," "purpose," "spirit" and "passion." These ideas are now seen as a vital component of workplace satisfaction, which in turn affects performance and productivity.

Meaning, spirit and passion—in a word, personal truth—are defined and experienced differently by each of us. The key to unlocking our personal truth is to know what we value. Articulating our guiding values puts us in touch with our passions—our *juice*—and it is this juice that fosters creativity, effectiveness, and our commitment to a larger purpose. Our passion lifts us above the tedium of rote tasks and bestows wonder and power to our lives at work. Clarifying our personal values also enables us to more precisely assess how well our personal vision, values and sense of purpose align with those of our organization. Without this alignment, we simply cannot do our best work, and we cannot contribute our unique gifts and talents with enthusiasm.

This simple workbook is a means for you to begin to clarify your values. It contains two sections. The first section is a presentation of twenty values that represent our inquiry into truth, meaning and passion. These value statements are intended to be catalysts for your process of discovery. There are questions at the end of each value statement to facilitate your exploration. Take as much time as you can to contemplate, consider, and reflect before answering them. If you need more space, use the pages provided at the end of the workbook.

The second section enables you to articulate, clarify and prioritize your own set of values and, from them, develop a set of behavioral commitments that will support you in "walking your own talk."

Don't be surprised if, over time, you find your viewpoint about certain values changing and evolving. This simply means that you are growing and learning. The important point is that you constantly refine your conscious understanding of the values that reflect your personal truth and passion. When we are not living from our values, from our heart, it is easy to become confused, conflicted, and sad. Our intent in providing this values workbook is that, as you use it, you may become clear of mind, peaceful of heart, and enthusiastic and passionate at work.

Love Your Work

Even if you are technically skillful and successful in terms of performance and income, that is not enough. You must love your chosen field of work. The French sculptor Auguste Rodin said, "The world will never be happy until all people have the souls of artists—that is, until they love their work." Loving your work means that, through it, you discover and express the most authentic and vibrant parts of yourself. The part of you that is passionate about what you do is the part that is able to find and contribute beauty and meaning to yourself and those around you.

This does not mean that some days aren't difficult and tedious. You may not like every aspect of a particular role, position, or project. But the overall experience and abiding commitment one can have towards one's work can be to have the soul of an artist. Through this commitment you become, in a way, an artist whose craft is working with passion and enthusiasm and joy.

Some people are only motivated by the outcome, the end result. They find little or no joy in the process, only in the satisfaction or recognition that comes with a successful outcome. This success is important, too, but how much better to be also motivated—moment by moment—by a love for your work, without regard to effect! Loving your work is about consciously recognizing the relationship between what you do, how you do it, and your longing for self-respect, recognition, personal satisfaction and growth. Loving your work is an expression of your deepest sense of meaning and purpose. It is truly a sharing of your heart.

What is it about your work that you love?

____

____

____

____

____

____

____

____

✠ How does your work reflect the deepest and most meaningful parts of yourself?

_____

_____

_____

_____

_____

_____

_____

_____

_____

✠ What changes could you make in your attitudes or in your work that would connect you more to what you love doing?

_____

_____

_____

_____

_____

_____

_____

_____

Be Conscious

Being conscious means being aware of those impulses, motives, and intentions that are behind, and are perhaps different from, what we present to others. For example, does what you say reflect what you mean, and are you truly aware of what you mean?

Conscious awareness is the moment-to-moment clarity of motive and intent. It is a balanced alignment among thought, word and action. One's values are broad guidelines; awareness is being deeply in touch with your thoughts and emotions every moment.

Without conscious awareness, we may become manipulative and deceitful—we may betray ourselves and our most noble aspirations, as well as exploit others. Without conscious awareness, we may live and work at the effect of unresolved conflicts from our past. We may let anger pollute our relationships; we may let unbridled ambition or an unexamined need for control and power undermine our work.

Being conscious is a commitment. This commitment to be conscious implies an ongoing process of self-inquiry, of discovery, of illuminating the unlit aspects of our subconscious that often drive us without our knowing it.

✖ At any given moment, how aware are you of the motives and intent behind your interactions?

_____

_____

_____

_____

_____

_____

_____

_____

_____

4

� How clear are you in communicating that intent to the people with whom you are interacting?

_____

_____

_____

_____

_____

_____

✖ Recall a time when you were not consciously aware of the motive or intent behind an interaction. What was the effect of the interaction? Was there a cost involved for anyone?

_____

_____

_____

_____

_____

✖ What steps could you take to become more conscious of your deepest impulses, desires, and fears?

_____

_____

_____

_____

_____

Act with Integrity

Integrity refers to what you know about your values and the degree to which you act in accord with them. Simply put, it reminds us that our actions ought to reflect what we deeply believe and feel is true for us in any given situation. A popular expression for integrity is to "walk our talk."

Integrity is the alignment of heart, body and mind. When we act from this alignment, we feel peace of mind. When we don't, we feel conflicted. This feeling of conflict is often a sign that we are betraying our heart—we are out of alignment.

In a broader sense, integrity refers to the level of consciousness with which you live and work. When you have integrity, others feel a certain assurance, or safety, in their dealings with you. A person with integrity has one face, not two or three. He or she has no hidden agenda, no dark and secretive undertones that cause others to be suspicious. This is particularly important if you supervise, manage or lead others because integrity inspires trust, confidence and loyalty. Integrity is the gold that guarantees the currency of our word, our actions, our intentions, and our commitments. When we lose our integrity, we lose our heart and our soul, as individuals and organizations.

✜ If integrity is the alignment of heart, body and mind, how would you assess your current level of integrity?

_____

_____

_____

_____

_____

_____

_____

_____

_____

_____

✠ How do you demonstrate integrity to the people with whom you work?

_____

_____

_____

_____

_____

_____

✠ What situations cause you to act counter to what you feel in your heart?

_____

_____

_____

_____

_____

_____

✠ What can you do to bring more integrity to these situations?

_____

_____

_____

_____

_____

The Larger Picture

We don't live or work in a vacuum. The work we do exists in the larger context of families, communities, societies and the world. Awareness of this requires that we become sensitive to the consequences of our work as it affects others. We should hold regular dialogues with ourselves and in our organizations about personal accountability, ethics and social responsibility. We ought to be very mindful of how our work touches others, directly and indirectly.

As a consequence of this broader view, we admit that we do not work and produce goods and services independent of their ripple effect. We can't be satisfied with profitability as the sole or primary justification for our work. We are inescapably linked and related to our communities and to the living eco-system of the world in which we live. We must then regulate our business by-products with an honest and sober reflection of their effect on the world.

❂ What is the larger context in which you do your work?

_____

_____

_____

_____

_____

_____

_____

_____

_____

_____

_____

_____

�֎ What do you do personally when something you or your organization wants to achieve is not in accord with the well-being of the greater context?

_____

_____

_____

_____

_____

_____

_____

_____

✖ How is this value relevant to the manner in which you currently work with others?

_____

_____

_____

_____

_____

_____

_____

_____

Respect and Appreciation

We don't know of anyone who truly likes to be mistreated, even though many of us accommodate this in our lives. In business situations, we often and easily rationalize mistreatment as part of the job, or fear that there will be some form of reprisal if we object to mistreatment by others. We tend to subordinate our desire for respect and appreciation in the face of this fear of "authority."

We each have to draw our lines—we each have to define and declare the ways in which we need to be treated in order for relationships to flourish. If we don't, we will always be at the mercy of how other people decide to treat us—we can then only "hope" for the best. This way of living puts us at the effect of others and erodes our self-esteem—we become habitual victims of our own lack of strength and clarity.

It is important to let others know that we expect to be treated with dignity, respect and appreciation at all times. Of course, we must at the same time earn people's respect and appreciation through appropriate attitudes and behaviors. When we practice relating to others with conscious awareness, consideration and integrity, we invite the respect and appreciation that we want from others.

Creating personal truth at work includes skillfully teaching others how we need to be treated so as to be able to be present without fear and to fully contribute our talents. We must also be ready and willing to treat others with the same respect and appreciation that we want from them. When we ask to be treated with dignity, when we earn the respect of others, and when we demonstrate our appreciation of others, we create a climate of goodwill and trust which in turn creates the possibility for exuberant and creative working relationships.

How would you assess the respect and appreciation you regularly show those with whom you work?

_____

_____

_____

_____

_____

_____

✖ If you are not treated with the respect and appreciation you need or expect, what can you do to clarify and define what that behavior should be?

_____

_____

_____

_____

_____

_____

✖ How might you communicate this expectation to the people with whom you work?

_____

_____

_____

_____

_____

_____

✖ If you are reluctant to communicate this expectation to the people with whom you work, why is that?

_____

_____

_____

_____

_____

_____

Be Who You Are

To be a real human being—to be natural and authentic—doesn't diminish your professionalism; it enhances it. Some people think you have to be aloof or appear special in some way in order to project an "expert" or "professional" aura. But if you have expertise, it will manifest in your work; you can still be a "real" person. People will appreciate you all the more for being real and accessible. Your expertise and track record may distinguish you from your colleagues; your humanness will bring you together.

Let others get to know you. This doesn't mean that you should bring your bronzed baby shoes to the office or spend hours talking about your childhood and your family and what you did between sixth and seventh grade. It simply means—be natural.

One way to determine how real you are in your work is to notice how much of a shift you experience between work and home. Of course there will be some shift, because your role changes. But you are not the role you play at work. If you often feel tense, sad, angry, frustrated or lonely at the end of the day, you may be suppressing your real self beneath a mask. If you live at work "authentically" you will not be crushed even at the end of a long and grueling day.

Being yourself implies that you welcome others to be their real selves in your presence. When you take the time to know the people with whom you work, you will be giving them a rare gift—the feeling of being heard, seen and acknowledged. Personalize your professional relationships so that people with whom you work feel you understand them, care about them, and have their well-being in mind. This means that you must be able to emotionally connect with people, enabling them to get to know you as you get to know them.

Being who you are allows you to express your joy and passion—and to demonstrate your uniqueness. It's very difficult to be creative, to give your best effort, when you are pretending to be someone you're not.

◳ Describe yourself when you are most authentic.

_____

_____

_____

_____

_____

✖ How does your description compare to "who you are" at work?

_____

_____

_____

_____

_____

_____

✖ If there are discrepancies, what can you do to reduce or eliminate them?

_____

_____

_____

_____

_____

✖ What do you think the people with whom you work would say about who you really are?

_____

_____

_____

_____

_____

_____

Interrogate Fear

Living passionately means to present our authentic self, which includes telling the truth of our thoughts and feelings, showing the full measure of our talents and abilities, reaching boldly for imaginative solutions, doing what has never been done, demonstrating our uniqueness. When we live this way, we live in accord with our deepest currents of truth. We experience a freedom, and a flow of wonder and exhilaration.

We don't always live like this. Sometimes a fear or doubt will get in the way. It is a rare day at work that we do not bargain with our fears on behalf of our true self-expression. It is not uncommon for fear to end up with the better deal. If our fears and doubts win a particular negotiation, wonder and exhilaration give way to anger, depression, and helplessness. When this happens, we usually feel as though there is nothing we can do but suffer silently. We become the victim of our silence and retreat into rationalizations, denial, or blame.

This is not a good situation for us or for others. When we fall prey to the silent suffering of helplessness, our soul withers and dies. On the other hand, when our authentic self-expression triumphs over fear, we become free. Freedom requires that we discover the ways in which we succumb to fear and jeopardize wonder and exhilaration.

We must name our fears as clearly as we can, so as to face them squarely. We must examine these fears to find their origins. We must examine what fear says will happen to determine whether those assertions are true. We must be very bold in our interrogation of fear—we simply can't believe the testimony of fear and doubt. We must expose its lies and false assumptions. This is the way to recover our truth and passion—this is the way to live and work with power, wonder, and joy.

Have you experienced a situation where you felt angry, depressed, or helpless due to fear? Name the fear that was behind this feeling.

✠ What does this fear say will happen? How can you determine if those assertions are true?

_____

_____

_____

_____

_____

_____

_____

_____

_____

✠ How can you prevent relinquishing your authentic self-expression to this fear?

_____

_____

_____

_____

_____

_____

_____

_____

_____

Communicate Clearly

Communication is the razor's edge between success and failure, respect and suspicion, cooperation and sabotage, joy and anger. When our communication with ourselves and with others is timely, clear, honest and skillful, there is nothing we cannot experience or achieve. When communication falters, breaks down, or stops, the game is over. Nothing can happen until communication resumes.

Always keep the people with whom you work appropriately informed about what you are doing, how you are doing it, and any other salient points important to a thriving and trusting relationship. Ask people if they need more information or support from you. Let them become familiar with your style, process, and methods of working. It will help them feel comfortable with you. When there is comfort and familiarity, there is a greater likelihood for a real sharing of thoughts and feelings and ideas—each person honestly offering his or her personal truth while accepting the personal truth of others will open powerful channels of caring and mutual understanding.

Let's be honest: There are always tense and worrisome situations at work. There isn't a person alive who does not flirt every day with self-suppression. Sometimes we think it's just easier to turn away, to let it go, to compromise. Other times we might want to exercise control by withholding or filtering communications. Some of us may communicate our emotional state by becoming impediments to the work—we find a way to stop the game—thereby covertly expressing some emotion that is difficult to express. It is quite common for people to fall into patterns of retreat and withholding when their feelings get hurt or they feel frustrated, unappreciated or afraid. We must all learn to recognize those tendencies that cause us to stop communicating, and then we can begin to work with them, to ease ourselves out of them.

Authentic self-expression is an absolute pre-requisite for creating personal truth. It is important to practice our communication skills and to develop mastery in this area. Clear and effective communication also develops self-confidence and builds trust. Honest and open communication creates the optimum climate for harmonious relationships and contributes to a climate of high achievement.

✵ Assess the current level of effectiveness of communication at your workplace.

_____

_____

_____

_____

� To what extent do you share information with others?

_____

_____

_____

_____

_____

_____

✖ What have you experienced when communication with others breaks down?

_____

_____

_____

_____

_____

_____

✖ What actions do you take (or need to take) to keep the channels of communication open?

_____

_____

_____

_____

_____

Emotional Maturity

This is one of the most important values because a lack of emotional maturity will manifest as all kinds of counter-productive behaviors. This value requires that you not project the shadow of unresolved personal issues on those with whom you work. Your work with colleagues may provoke deep and profound reactivity because of lingering tensions from childhood, or conflicts with parents or other authority figures. Try to avoid using your professional relationships to act out these issues and conflicts. It is important to be able to distinguish between personal issues that you may project onto a situation and what is a part of the situation itself.

However, when issues and conflicts do appear, deal with them, if possible in a way that both promotes the work and honors the relationship with your colleague. If you need to address a colleague's counter-productivity, do so with clarity, directness, and a sensitivity to the possible motives for his or her behavior. If you notice that your own reactions are counter-productive, become clear about your own behavior and make the necessary adjustments. Do not allow your own intra-personal work to masquerade as interpersonal clashes.

Emotional maturity means being committed to inner growth in a responsible manner. This value and the value *Be Conscious* feed and nurture each other. Consciousness and emotional maturity are not taught in business or professional courses, but they are at least as important as knowing how to build a decision tree or interpret a P&L statement. We think they are much more important because our behavior is often driven by our emotional state. The more we master our emotions, the more we intelligently manage our behavior.

How do you deal with your "emotional reactivity" to situations and relationships?

_____

_____

_____

_____

_____

_____

_____

�֎ What personal issues have you noticed that you project on situations with colleagues?

_____

_____

_____

_____

_____

_____

_____

_____

✖ What do you do on a regular basis to face and resolve your own issues and conflicts?

_____

_____

_____

_____

_____

_____

_____

_____

_____

Gain the Cooperation of Others

People with whom you work may not always be as cooperative and attentive to you, your priorities, or your needs as you would like. It may feel as though they are creating obstacles. Try not to allow others' uncooperativeness or roadblocks to interfere with your work.

Learn how to gain the cooperation and attention of others. This is a critical piece of learning how to manage professional relationships. If we react with immaturity and anger or let our frustration get the better of us, we have simply created more difficulty. Learn to manage yourself and others so that all are working together from an attentive and cooperative stance.

This value requires self-restraint. We may often have to negotiate and compromise in our professional relationships. There is nothing wrong with this. We must be committed to finding common ground. Individually we must become the inspirational means through which others will want to cooperate with us.

Think about how you work with others. Are you more involved in reacting to obstacles, creating obstacles, or finding common ground?

�֎ What do you think your colleagues would say about your commitment to finding common ground?

_____

_____

_____

_____

_____

✖ How do you work with others to gain their cooperation?

_____

_____

_____

_____

_____

✖ What might you do differently in working to gain the cooperation of others?

_____

_____

_____

_____

_____

Listen! Huh? LISTEN!

Listening is vital in every human endeavor. It doesn't mean hearing, which happens more or less because we have ears. Listening is a skill that requires learning and practice—it requires focus and attention.

By truly listening we establish the field in which our relationships unfold. Listening is the means by which we perceive and receive the reality of others. Listening allows you to effectively relate to others as they say they are, not as who you think or guess they are. Listening involves opening your total being to another's total being. To really listen means that you are present, attentive and alive, not thinking ahead about how you'll respond or daydreaming about what you're going to have for lunch. Learning how to listen is an enormous undertaking, the mastery of which will continue throughout your life.

Most if not all misunderstandings can be significantly resolved through listening. Listening gives birth to understanding, understanding to empathy, empathy to clarity, clarity to generosity. Being generous in our relationships will go a long way towards developing trust, mutual understanding, cooperation and respect. Skillful listening also helps us gather useful navigational information from which we can course-correct our behavior or direction. We are more apt to land our plane on the correct runway and avoid catastrophic collisions.

Run, don't walk, to the nearest bookstore or training center and begin the journey of learning how to listen.

Think of the best listener you know. What are the characteristics or behaviors that enable this person to be such an effective listener?

____

____

____

____

____

____

____

____

�֍ What are your three best listening qualities?

_____

_____

_____

_____

_____

✖ How could becoming a better listener enhance your professional ability?

_____

_____

_____

_____

_____

✖ What listening qualities would you like to develop? What is your plan for developing these qualities?

_____

_____

_____

_____

_____

_____

Add Value

This is simple. Always find a way to give more than the most that is expected of you. This *value added* attitude builds goodwill and appreciation among your colleagues. In a way, adding value is a kind of exuberant expression of your love of the work.

This value refers to not standing only at the edge of your duties, responsibilities and commitments, but to taking an extra step. Give more than the minimum, more than is required. This value will serve you by causing you to stretch, to grow, to extend yourself beyond limits imposed by you or others.

Many of us keep too exact an accounting of what we do compared to what we get. This attitude tends to suppress our exuberance and creativity, as well as the joy we should be experiencing from full participation in our chosen work. If you love your work, if you are getting respect and appreciation, if you are co-creating the playing field, you will naturally want to pump more of yourself into your work. Adding value does not imply being a doormat or workaholic. It has more to do with pretending that every day is Thanksgiving or Christmas.

When you give more than is expected, more than the minimum required, don't make a big deal out of it. Think of it as good karma. Sometimes it will come back to you, but don't do it for that reason. Do it to practice generosity of spirit. It's contagious!

✳ What are some examples of when you have given more than was expected?

_____

_____

_____

_____

_____

_____

_____

_____

_____

� What are some opportunities in a current project to give more than is expected?

_____

_____

_____

_____

_____

_____

_____

_____

✖ What might prevent you from providing this added service?

_____

_____

_____

_____

_____

_____

_____

_____

Keep Fit and Healthy

A component of our ability to operate at an optimum professional level requires fitness and health of body, mind and spirit. Our capacity to see clearly and deal effectively with situations and relationships is directly impacted by our fitness and health. Some professionals pride themselves on being chronically exhausted. What are they trying to prove?

Yes, from time to time you'll have an assignment that for one reason or another is going to take everything from you and you will feel empty and tired. But if you are committed to your health and fitness, this will be an infrequent occurrence and you will be able to recuperate quickly. If you don't keep your body, mind and spirit in good shape, you impede your effectiveness and your capacity for joy. And please, don't blame your work for your lack of fitness. Remember, you are a co-creator in the playing field. The fitness and health you achieve and maintain will support your work life. You must have energy and vitality to experience fulfillment at work, as is true for all areas of your life.

One way to stay healthy is to be committed to personal growth and learning. Learn about yourself and what you need in terms of balance, exercise, diet, recreation, time with friends and family, and participation in social, cultural and volunteer activities. One's health is a function of living a full, rich, rewarding life. It is a gift that we must give to ourselves, so that we can truly give ourselves to others and to our work.

What is your experience of the relationship between fitness and a satisfying work life?

_____

_____

_____

_____

_____

_____

_____

_____

�֎ How fit are you? What do you do on a regular basis to remain healthy and energetic?

_____

_____

_____

_____

_____

_____

✖ How conscious and careful are you about nutrition and exercise?

_____

_____

_____

_____

_____

✖ What do you do on a regular basis to stay healthy in mind and spirit?

_____

_____

_____

_____

_____

_____

"I Don't Know"

In business, we are often afraid of saying "I don't know." We think it might be a sign of weakness or inability. We might be afraid that others will think less of us. Saying "I don't know" does not undermine your expertise or professionalism—it emphasizes your humanity. Being professional and being human are not mutually exclusive. Also, saying *I don't know* means you are on the frontier of your knowledge and skill and experience, which in turn means that you are pushing hard on the boundary of the familiar and conventional.

"I don't know" is fantastic. You are about to discover a piece of the unknown and become a bigger and wiser person. In not knowing, you are free to see what is there in front of you that you haven't seen before. You can let your eyes see, and your ears hear, and your heart feel in ways not limited or constrained by the past. You can let your intuition sense deeply into the truth of a situation because you are not all cluttered up with what you "know."

When it comes to meeting adversity, solving problems, resolving interpersonal tensions, being able to say "I don't know" opens the door to new possibilities.

If saying "I don't know" is difficult for you, why is that?

_____

_____

_____

_____

_____

_____

_____

_____

_____

_____

_____

Can you think of a time when a greater willingness to admit you didn't know something would have made a positive difference? What got in your way?

How is this value relevant to the manner in which you work?

Be Accountable

Being accountable is recognizing that you always have the opportunity to create your own experience. We may sometimes think that our colleagues or the tensions and difficulties inherent in our work are responsible for our experience. Regardless of what is happening or what we'd like to believe, the basic and incontrovertible fact is that we have total freedom in terms of how we choose to experience what happens. We cannot always control outer events, but we do always generate our experience of and response to these events.

We can create our own experience; we can choose to be joyful, enthusiastic and positive, or we can be depressed, resentful and negative. These choices are not a function of what is happening. They are a function of our level of accountability for our own experience.

Accountability extends beyond our experience and includes a willingness to see our role in situations. You will sometimes encounter difficulties in your work—people won't listen to you, balls get dropped, tempers flare, deadlines are missed, and so on. Before blaming something or someone else, try to see what your role might be in the situation—how you might be a component of the difficulty.

When problems arise, assess the clarity of your motives, preparation, commitment, communication and, especially, your emotional reactivity. Quite often we can discover something about ourselves—our intentions and behavior—that has contributed to the problem, such that when we correct that within our own self, the problem is significantly altered.

❇ Do you feel your experience is determined by your inner response or by outer circumstances?

_____

_____

_____

_____

_____

_____

�֎ What can you do, independent of circumstances, to create more of what you want to experience?

_____

_____

_____

_____

_____

_____

✖ When something goes wrong, where do you look for clues as to the source of the problem?

_____

_____

_____

_____

_____

_____

✖ What is your own personal process for being accountable in your professional relationships?

_____

_____

_____

_____

_____

_____

Use Your Intuition

Intuition is like lightning: You can't capture it in a bottle. Even if you could, you would be taming what is essentially wild.

Intuition refers to an aspect of our consciousness that is not constrained by the past, by reason, or by cause-and-effect. It is a sudden, spontaneous knowing that is a function of each moment or situation. Intuition allows us to know things we didn't know we knew.

Intuition is like magic. Your willingness to explore the frontier of your own powers of mind and consciousness are essential. Don't succumb to being only rational. Perhaps Don Quixote was teaching his friend about intuition when he said, "Facts, my dear Sancho, are the enemies of Truth." It is okay to color outside the lines of convention. In fact, it's important that we learn to do this. This aspect of our potential is the rich field in which amazing flowers of creativity and invention appear, much like a magician pulls paper flowers out of thin air. This world of intuition links us to the world of spirit, and the world of spirit in turn links us to everyone and everything.

Developing this capacity pays big dividends in our ability to listen and respond, to be creative and innovative, to solve problems, and to overcome adversity. Our intuition is eminently practical and useful; it is also a conduit of personal passion and clarity. We can apply our listening skills to our own deep self and learn to hear subtle messages of guidance and insight. Many of our values will come from the quiet reflection that intuition often requires of us.

How willing are you to listen to and trust your intuition?

_____

_____

_____

_____

_____

_____

_____

_____

�֍ What might be getting in the way of listening to and trusting your intuition?

_____

_____

_____

_____

_____

_____

✷ Recall a situation in which you consciously followed your intuition. How did it feel? What was the outcome?

_____

_____

_____

_____

_____

_____

✷ How do you develop your intuitive self?

_____

_____

_____

_____

_____

It Wouldn't Kill You to Laugh

If love is the universal language, then laughter must be its most familiar dialect. Laughter allows us to connect with people and share the joys and sorrows of life's journey that we are all taking together. Laughter is an expression of joy, passion and empathy. You don't have to be a clown—just be willing to see the humor in things. Laughter is also a wonderful way to dissipate tension and reduce stress.

How many meetings have you been to that were tedious beyond belief? How many presentations have you sat through that almost killed you to do so? How many planning sessions have you been a part of, even though you could barely breathe in the humorless atmosphere?

Be quite ready to laugh, to enjoy, to smile at the ironies of living. This doesn't compromise your professionalism, nor does it prevent high-level performance. In fact, without laughter, how long can you endure any situation? We can't imagine going through a day without laughing at something. Laughter is more comforting than chocolate, and has far fewer calories!

What place do you think laughter has in a "professional" relationship?

_____

_____

_____

_____

_____

_____

_____

_____

_____

_____

_____

�젰 How easily do you laugh and express delight with your professional colleagues?

_____

_____

_____

_____

_____

✻ What situations can you recall in which humor might have led to a more positive outcome?

_____

_____

_____

_____

_____

✻ How is this value relevant to the manner in which you currently work with others?

_____

_____

_____

_____

_____

Be Responsive

Like it or not, power games are frequently played at work. Some people do things which they think enhance their stature or self-importance, like not returning calls promptly, or being terminally unavailable or late, or denying access to crucial information. Sad but true, we often experience being ignored, blown off, or treated with impatience or disdain. Please don't do this. Be responsive to people!

Being responsive means being on time and available regardless of what else is going on. If you can't give someone the attention they need because of a legitimate conflict with other priorities, tell them that and arrange a time when you can respond to them.

While it's true that we all have more than we can do on any given day, we must still be responsive to others. It is a matter of attitude, not time. To have someone be enthusiastically responsive to you is one of the most refreshing experiences one can have in the business world. People will want to work with you if they have the experience of being responded to with courtesy, interest and care.

Being responsive also means listening with your entire body. It implies that you are present, attentive, interested and enthusiastic. As with all of these values, the more you practice them, the more others will be inspired to practice them. Someone has to be first. Be responsive, pay attention, do what you say you will do, and appreciate others for doing the same. This is a value that can transform a work place quicker than a snap of the fingers. It is an instant soup for those hungry for connection, respect, and cooperation with others.

Are you responsive to those with whom you work? If not, why?

�֎ In your organization, how do you treat your internal customers compared to your external customers?

_____

_____

_____

_____

_____

_____

✖ If there is a difference in your treatment, why is that?

_____

_____

_____

_____

_____

✖ What recent situations may have had a different outcome if you had been more responsive?

_____

_____

_____

_____

_____

_____

Enjoy Differences

To be ethnocentric means to arbitrarily believe in the superiority of our own attitudes, beliefs and customs over those of people who do not share our various racial, religious or cultural affiliations. We all see the world through the filters of our beliefs, and these beliefs are not *better than,* only *different from*. Beneath the surface differences among people is the common human desire for peace, happiness and fulfillment.

The more open you are to the differences others bring to your experience, the more you discover fresh and fascinating facets of yourself. In choosing not to be ethnocentric, but instead to be influenced and impacted by others and to discover new facets of yourself, you learn how to enjoy—to celebrate—differences.

In the landscape of today's business world, we do not have to travel any farther than the next cubicle or office to experience people who are different from us in some important way. What and how we each "see" has validity. The customs, manners and perceptions that differentiate one person from another are the very differences that can strengthen a group's enterprise.

How are the people with whom you work different from you?

✖ What do you let get in the way of welcoming and appreciating the perceptions, ideas and viewpoints of those whose race, religion or culture differs from your own?

_____

_____

_____

_____

_____

_____

_____

_____

✖ How is this value relevant to the manner in which you currently work with others?

_____

_____

_____

_____

_____

_____

_____

_____

Gratitude

To be grateful implies that we try to see the bounty and abundance in our life. True, we might want more, but that is no reason to not appreciate what we do have. We too often focus on what is negative, incomplete or unfulfilled.

Gratitude is an antidote for that; it is an attitude of the heart in which beauty, appreciation and humility brighten one's daily experience. It means acknowledging others for their effort, their kindness, their good works. A simple, heartfelt thank you to someone will create beautiful reverberations. See what happens in your business environment, in your relationships, and in your own experience of living when you practice gratitude.

One way to begin the practice of gratitude is to notice, at the end of the work day, the interactions and occurrences for which you can be grateful. It may have been someone's good humor in a stressful situation, someone's extra effort in completing a report, or your satisfaction of having worked successfully with a difficult customer or colleague.

This quick and simple practice when done regularly will begin to transform your perspective. It will enable you to value your colleagues and work experience in a more positive manner. It can also become the basis upon which you communicate your appreciation to others for their contribution. What a nice pattern to establish—you close the workday by noticing your gratitude and begin the next day by communicating to others your appreciation of them!

How do you currently practice gratitude?

�֍ What do you let get in the way of sharing your gratitude with others?

_____

_____

_____

_____

_____

_____

_____

_____

✖ For what do you currently feel gratitude, and with whom would you like to share this?

_____

_____

_____

_____

_____

_____

_____

_____

_____

By working through the previous pages you have completed a portion of the inquiry into your values. Now you have the opportunity to transform that inquiry into a personal articulation of your own guiding values.

The following pages provide the space to record your own set of values—ones that reflect your personal truth and passion. You may certainly select, prioritize, and modify any of those values from the previous section that are meaningful and relevant to you. But we encourage you to create your set of values with as much originality as possible. Make them yours. Put your unique fingerprints on each value. In this way, you will truly know your heart and its passions and truth, and you will be able to live consciously and clearly from them.

You may want to copy your completed set of values and keep them in your workspace or daily calendar book. Having them available to review periodically will keep them more alive and present for you.

Also, the values you record today may change and evolve over time. Plan to revisit them occasionally with the intent of revising them based on your increased consciousness of your personal truth and passion.

Enjoy the journey this practice provides you in becoming clear of mind, peaceful of heart, and enthusiastic and passionate at work.

MY VALUE ONE

____

Summary of Value:____

Specific behaviors I need to practice and/or actions I need to take to put this value into practice.

Current situations that could be positively impacted by practicing this value.

_____

�֎ Summary of Value:_____

_____

_____

_____

_____

✖ Specific behaviors I need to practice and/or actions I need to take to put this value into practice.

_____

_____

_____

_____

_____

_____

_____

_____

✖ Current situations that could be positively impacted by practicing this value.

_____

_____

_____

_____

_____

_____

_____

�֍ Summary of Value:_____

_____

_____

_____

✖ Specific behaviors I need to practice and/or actions I need to take to put this value into practice.

_____

_____

_____

_____

_____

_____

✖ Current situations that could be positively impacted by practicing this value.

_____

_____

_____

_____

_____

_____

____

Summary of Value:____

Specific behaviors I need to practice and/or actions I need to take to put this value into practice.

Current situations that could be positively impacted by practicing this value.

____

Summary of Value:

Specific behaviors I need to practice and/or actions I need to take to put this value into practice.

Current situations that could be positively impacted by practicing this value.

_____

✠ Summary of Value:_____

_____

_____

_____

_____

✠ Specific behaviors I need to practice and/or actions I need to take to put this value into practice.

_____

_____

_____

_____

_____

_____

_____

✠ Current situations that could be positively impacted by practicing this value.

_____

_____

_____

_____

_____

_____

_____

✠ Summary of Value:_____

_____

_____

_____

_____

✠ Specific behaviors I need to practice and/or actions I need to take to put this value into practice.

_____

_____

_____

_____

_____

_____

_____

_____

✠ Current situations that could be positively impacted by practicing this value.

_____

_____

_____

_____

_____

_____

_____

_____

✖ Summary of Value:_____

_____

_____

_____

_____

✖ Specific behaviors I need to practice and/or actions I need to take to put this value into practice.

_____

_____

_____

_____

_____

_____

_____

_____

✖ Current situations that could be positively impacted by practicing this value.

_____

_____

_____

_____

_____

_____

�֎ Summary of Value:_____

_____

_____

_____

_____

✖ Specific behaviors I need to practice and/or actions I need to take to put this value into practice.

_____

_____

_____

_____

_____

_____

_____

_____

✖ Current situations that could be positively impacted by practicing this value.

_____

_____

_____

_____

_____

_____

_____

_____

✠ Summary of Value:_____

_____

_____

_____

_____

✠ Specific behaviors I need to practice and/or actions I need to take to put this value into practice.

_____

_____

_____

_____

_____

_____

_____

_____

✠ Current situations that could be positively impacted by practicing this value.

_____

_____

_____

_____

_____

_____

_____

✖ Summary of Value:_____

_____

_____

_____

✖ Specific behaviors I need to practice and/or actions I need to take to put this value into practice.

_____

_____

_____

_____

_____

_____

_____

✖ Current situations that could be positively impacted by practicing this value.

_____

_____

_____

_____

_____

_____

____

Summary of Value: ________________________________

____

____

____

____

Specific behaviors I need to practice and/or actions I need to take to put this value into practice.

____

____

____

____

____

____

____

____

Current situations that could be positively impacted by practicing this value.

____

____

____

____

____

____

____

_____

�֎ Summary of Value:_____

_____

_____

_____

_____

✖ Specific behaviors I need to practice and/or actions I need to take to put this value into practice.

_____

_____

_____

_____

_____

_____

_____

_____

✖ Current situations that could be positively impacted by practicing this value.

_____

_____

_____

_____

_____

_____

_____

_____

⊞ Summary of Value:_____

_____

_____

_____

_____

⊞ Specific behaviors I need to practice and/or actions I need to take to put this value into practice.

_____

_____

_____

_____

_____

_____

_____

⊞ Current situations that could be positively impacted by practicing this value.

_____

_____

_____

_____

_____

_____

✠ Summary of Value:_____

_____

_____

_____

_____

✠ Specific behaviors I need to practice and/or actions I need to take to put this value into practice.

_____

_____

_____

_____

_____

_____

_____

_____

_____

✠ Current situations that could be positively impacted by practicing this value.

_____

_____

_____

_____

_____

_____

_____

_____

�֍ Summary of Value:_____

_____

_____

_____

_____

�֍ Specific behaviors I need to practice and/or actions I need to take to put this value into practice.

_____

_____

_____

_____

_____

_____

_____

�֍ Current situations that could be positively impacted by practicing this value.

_____

_____

_____

_____

_____

_____

_____

⊠ Summary of Value:_____

_____

_____

_____

_____

⊠ Specific behaviors I need to practice and/or actions I need to take to put this value into practice.

_____

_____

_____

_____

_____

_____

_____

⊠ Current situations that could be positively impacted by practicing this value.

_____

_____

_____

_____

_____

_____

_____

✵ Summary of Value:_____

_____

_____

_____

_____

✵ Specific behaviors I need to practice and/or actions I need to take to put this value into practice.

_____

_____

_____

_____

_____

_____

_____

_____

✵ Current situations that could be positively impacted by practicing this value.

_____

_____

_____

_____

_____

_____

_____

�֎ Summary of Value:_____

_____

_____

_____

_____

✖ Specific behaviors I need to practice and/or actions I need to take to put this value into practice.

_____

_____

_____

_____

_____

_____

_____

_____

✖ Current situations that could be positively impacted by practicing this value.

_____

_____

_____

_____

_____

_____

_____

✠ Summary of Value:_____

_____

_____

_____

_____

✠ Specific behaviors I need to practice and/or actions I need to take to put this value into practice.

_____

_____

_____

_____

_____

_____

_____

_____

✠ Current situations that could be positively impacted by practicing this value.

_____

_____

_____

_____

_____

_____

MY VALUE

_____

�֎ Summary of Value:_____

_____

_____

_____

_____

✖ Specific behaviors I need to practice and/or actions I need to take to put this value into practice.

_____

_____

_____

_____

_____

_____

_____

_____

✖ Current situations that could be positively impacted by practicing this value.

_____

_____

_____

_____

_____

_____

_____

MY VALUE

_____

�֍ Summary of Value:_____

_____

_____

_____

✖ Specific behaviors I need to practice and/or actions I need to take to put this value into practice.

_____

_____

_____

_____

_____

_____

✖ Current situations that could be positively impacted by practicing this value.

_____

_____

_____

_____

_____

_____

_____

✠ Summary of Value:_____

_____

_____

_____

_____

✠ Specific behaviors I need to practice and/or actions I need to take to put this value into practice.

_____

_____

_____

_____

_____

_____

_____

_____

✠ Current situations that could be positively impacted by practicing this value.

_____

_____

_____

_____

_____

_____

_____

_____

✠ Summary of Value:_____

_____

_____

_____

_____

✠ Specific behaviors I need to practice and/or actions I need to take to put this value into practice.

_____

_____

_____

_____

_____

_____

_____

_____

✠ Current situations that could be positively impacted by practicing this value.

_____

_____

_____

_____

_____

_____

�֎ Summary of Value:_____

_____

_____

_____

_____

✖ Specific behaviors I need to practice and/or actions I need to take to put this value into practice.

_____

_____

_____

_____

_____

_____

_____

_____

✖ Current situations that could be positively impacted by practicing this value.

_____

_____

_____

_____

_____

_____

_____

NOTES

ROBERT RABBIN—author, speaker, and consultant— has had a lifelong interest in the nature of the human mind and consciousness. In 1969 he began the practice self-inquiry to cultivate inner awareness and clarity. In the early 1970s he continued his explorations of self, mind, reality and consciousness while traveling throughout Europe and the Middle East. In 1973 he trekked overland to India, where he met a meditation master with whom he studied for ten years.

In 1985, Robert began sharing his insights with others in the form of meditative inquiry dialogues, which he continues to offer interested groups of people throughout the country. He is also an executive advisor who is consulted by leaders from a broad range of companies and organizations. Rob has designed and produced unique corporate retreats for individuals, teams, and entire companies, in which his clients can explore the frontiers of their own capacities and consciousness.

Robert is the author of *The Sacred Hub: Living in Your Real Self* (The Crossing Press, 1996), and is a contributor to the anthology *Leadership in a New Era* (New Leaders Press, 1994). He writes "The Corporate Mystic," a regular column published in the boutique newsletter *The New Leaders*. His articles and interviews are published internationally in newspapers, magazines, and journals such as *Creation Spirituality, Noetic Sciences Review, Yoga Journal, Inner Directions Journal, New Frontier, Napra ReView, New World News,* and *World Business Academy Perspectives.*

He also wrote and produced *Brilliant Business: A Road Map to the 21st Century,* the landmark film about passion, spirit, and freedom in corporate America.

Robert is a frequent speaker to groups in the spiritual, academic, and business communities. He has presented his original insights as a member of conference panels and in lively, interactive seminars to such groups as the Institute of Noetic Sciences, John F. Kennedy University, and the California Institute of Integral Studies. He has also been a guest on numerous radio shows, such as "Connecting Point" in Los Angeles; "Seeing Beyond" in San Francisco; and "Beyond Reason" in Nashville.

For more information about Robert and his work, please contact him at:

ROBERT RABBIN
2629 Manhattan Avenue, Suite 192
Hermosa Beach, CA 90254

Phone: 310.535.1768
E-mail: robrabbin@infoasis.com
Web Site: www.robrabbin.com

JO HILLYARD— educator, manager, and consultant— has worked with executives, managers and employees at all levels to improve overall employee effectiveness. Her work always maintains a focus on raising people's awareness of how they interact with others. Her unique instructional methodology features a "learner focused" approach that increases learner involvement in the training process. Her programs in the areas of performance management and customer service provide opportunities for individuals to clarify their purpose and to better understand how they impact others. She especially loves working with trainers to clarify their own purposefulness, and to expand their ability to facilitate learning.

After several years in the field of public education, Jo pursued a broader perspective on the *business* of education by joining Ginn and Company, then an educational publishing division of Xerox Corporation. She spent eight years in the publishing and sales side of the industry as a consultant and training manager, expanding her expertise in learning process, instructional design, training, sales, service, and managing people.

In the early 80s, the phenomenon of adults learning a new technology—personal computers—drew Jo to Know How, Inc., an early entry in the field of third party computer training, where she developed new methodologies as Vice President of Curriculum and Training. This eventually led her to direct technical, end user and sales training for a software manufacturer in Silicon Valley. In 1985, she seized the opportunity to fulfill her dream of starting her own business working with companies to analyze performance and to design and implement training solutions.

As President of Hillyard Associates, Inc., she is also a sought-after consultant in the design and manufacture of "off-the-shelf" as well as customized training products. Jo has conducted over 1,100 skills training and train-the-trainer seminars, written over 55 training courses and taught workshops in instructional strategies at UC Berkeley and San Francisco State University. She served on the Curriculum Advisory Board at UC Berkeley for the Certificate Program in *Training and Human Resource Development.*

For more information about Jo and her work, please contact her at:

JO HILLYARD
Hillyard Associates, Inc.
Phone: 650.345.0242
Fax: 650.345.4552
E-mail: jshinc@concentric.net